VIDEO GAMES, YES OR NO

WITHDRAWN

Erin Palmer

Rourke
Educational Media

rourkeeducationalmedia.com

Scan for Related Titles
and Teacher Resources

Teaching Focus:
Concepts of Print- Have students find capital letters and punctuation in a sentence. Ask students to explain the purpose for using them in a sentence.

Before Reading:

Building Academic Vocabulary and Background Knowledge
Before reading a book, it is important to set the stage for your child or students by using pre-reading strategies. This will help them develop their vocabulary, increase their reading comprehension, and make connections across the curriculum.

1. *Read the title and look at the cover. Let's make predictions about what this book will be about.*
2. *Take a picture walk by talking about the pictures/photographs in the book. Implant the vocabulary as you take the picture walk. Be sure to talk about the text features such as headings, Table of Contents, glossary, bolded words, captions, charts/diagrams, or Index.*
3. *Have students read the first page of text with you then have students read the remaining text.*
4. *Strategy Talk – use to assist students while reading.*
   - *Get your mouth ready*
   - *Look at the picture*
   - *Think…does it make sense*
   - *Think…does it look right*
   - *Think…does it sound right*
   - *Chunk it – by looking for a part you know*
5. *Read it again.*
6. *After reading the book complete the activities below.*

Content Area Vocabulary
Use glossary words in a sentence.
argument
negative
opinions
opponents
pastime
proponents

After Reading:

Comprehension and Extension Activity
After reading the book, work on the following questions with your child or students in order to check their level of reading comprehension and content mastery.

1. *What would be good habits to have when playing video games? (Summarize)*
2. *In what ways can video games set a bad example? (Infer)*
3. *How can video games keep you from making friends? How can video games help you make friends? (Asking questions)*
4. *Do you play video games that teach you new skills or information? Share with us. (Text to self connection)*

Extension Activity
Do you play video games? Think about all the games you play on a console, computer, or tablet. How much time do you spend playing them? For one week record how much time you are spending playing a video game each day. Then create a graph that shows how much time was spent playing video games each day. Which day did you play the most? Why? Which day did you play the least? Why? What are some ways you can limit the time spent playing video games?

Table of Contents

Introduction

Video games are a popular **pastime** for children and adults, but many people have different **opinions** about them.

Video games may have good and bad elements.

An opinion is the way a person feels about an issue or question. When people have different opinions, it doesn't mean one person is wrong and the other is right.

Just like you and a friend may not have the same favorite color, some people may have different opinions about whether video games are positive or **negative**.

When you learn about both sides of a subject, you can form your own opinion and make your own **argument**.

About 60 percent of Americans play video games. Most of them play at least an hour per week.

Arguments for Video Games

For a lot of people, video games can be a source of fun, entertainment, and education.

Video games can be played online, bringing people together from all over the world.

Video games can help people learn new skills. Some video games teach pilots how to fly!

Researchers discovered that some workers learn more and forget less when they are trained using video games.

Video games can teach you how to use different strategies to solve a problem.

Some video games even teach kids how to design their own video games.

Video game **proponents** encourage schools to use video games in lessons about math, reading, science, history, and other subjects.

Sometimes people are so busy having fun playing video games, they don't notice they are learning too!

Arguments against Video Games

Many people think video games set a bad example.

Unlike TV shows or movies that sometimes show bad things, a video game player controls what happens.

People who play a lot of violent video games may become more hostile, some researchers say.

If you see a fight in a movie, you are only watching it. If you play a video game, your choices make the fight happen.

whoosh

Is the person who plays a video game making a bad choice if they hurt a character in a game?

Video game **opponents** argue that games can promote unhealthy habits, since they are often played while sitting still indoors.

Some health experts say looking at a screen for long periods of time can be bad for your eyes.

Some people think video games keep people from making friends because they are too busy playing inside alone.

You Decide

There are a lot of things to keep in mind when forming an opinion about video games.

Think about the issues on both sides and decide what the most important points are to consider before making your decision.

So, what do you think? Are you for or against video games?